# Queensland by invitation

*Queensland by Invitation* is an initiative to focus the attention of Queenslanders on the attributes that make Queensland a unique, smart, vibrant and special place to live, work, travel in and enjoy.

The Premier of Queensland, The Hon Peter Beattie MP, personally invited 400 Queenslanders from all walks of life to present 'their view' of contemporary Queensland in words and pictures.

The 100 entries chosen by a special selection panel reflect the geographic, multicultural and demographic diversity of Queensland.

It is fitting that the Premier will launch the publication on Queensland Day 2002. Queensland Day acknowledges the State's birth. It was on 6 June 1859 that Queen Victoria gave her approval and signed Letters Patent to establish the new colony of Queensland.

Queensland then became a self-governing colony with its own Governor, a nominated Legislative Council and an elected Legislative Assembly. Queensland Day now allows Queenslanders to celebrate their uniqueness and successes and to recognise their achievers.

The day now also includes the annual announcement of five Queensland Greats.

**Queensland**
Government

The publication is celebration of all that is great about Queensland.

# Queensland by invitation

# Roll of Honour

## Lead

Golden Circle Limited

Griffith University

Ipswich City Council

South Bank Corporation/South Bank Business Association

The University of Queensland

## Major

Brisbane Marketing

Ergon Energy Pty Ltd

Fisher & Paykel Appliances Limited

Fuji Xerox Australia

Golden Casket Lottery Corporation Limited

Queensland Investment Corporation

Royal National Association

Tarong Energy Corporation Limited

The Riviera Group

Warner Village Theme Parks

## Contributing

ABN AMRO Morgans Ltd

Australian Magnesium Corporation Limited

Bank of Queensland

Devine Limited

Dreamworld

Energex

George Patterson Bates

InterGen (Australia) Pty Ltd

Jupiters Limited

Macarthur Coal Limited

Nerada Tea Pty Ltd

Origin Energy Limited

Reliance Worldwide

SunWater

Townsville Enterprise Limited

WorkCover Queensland

Yellow Cabs (Queensland) Pty Ltd

# Contents

# Queensland by invitation

When I announced the concept of this book I said that I wanted the rest of Australia and the world to know just how great Queensland really is. We have something very special here in Queensland and it deserves to be preserved and recorded in history.

*Queensland by Invitation* is a book about Queensland from the point of view of everyday Queenslanders. It is a snapshot of the Queensland way of life, its people, their places and their future in the Smart State.

I've invited 400 Queenslanders from all walks of life to contribute to the project and 100 have been chosen to present their own words and pictures about what Queensland means to them. That way, we are revealing the real heart of Queensland and its people.

People were asked to use their imagination and decide on the picture and words that evoke their story and their place in the world at this time.

Queensland is the greatest place in the world in which to live.

But in choosing just one image to sum it all up I decided I would select a jacaranda.

It's an example of the spectacular bright colours and vibrancy that Queensland has to offer while at the same time offering beauty and tranquillity. It heralds the start of summer and the return of beach life and barbecues.

The jacaranda trees outside Parliament House, Brisbane

In particular, I chose the jacaranda which stands outside the magnificent sandstone facade of Parliament House, the seat of democracy in Queensland, which helps to guard our freedoms and our envied lifestyle.

In doing so I was being doubly patriotic, because Parliament House and its beautiful jacaranda are in my electorate of Brisbane Central. For all these reasons, the parliamentary jacaranda is my choice of picture for what Queensland means to me.

Peter Beattie MP
Premier and Minister for Trade

# Quintessential Queensland

## Part 1

We love our local park, but over last summer the whole billabong was choked by salvinia weed. **The neighbours rallied** and local council sent in bulldozers for a cooperative cleanup. Now it is alive again. We restocked and nurtured appropriate fish, and more of us are caring for the billabong than ever before. We've met new neighbours and the council team in the process, and our children are continuing to learn about their natural backyard.

And it all came about because of a common community attitude: working together to enhance our lifestyle and our natural environment. That's Queensland to me.

Russell Boswell. Brogla Park, Brolga Street, Kewarra Beach. 18 November 2001, 5pm.

Mike Burgess. Quicksilver at Agincourt Reef, July 2000.

The magnificent Great Barrier Reef World Heritage Area provides a wonderful legacy for the people of Queensland. It is a **paradise that offers an endless sense of excitement,** fascination and enjoyment for locals and visitors from all walks of life. There is also the opportunity to derive substantial economic and social advantages if this resource is wisely used. With these benefits comes an awesome responsibility to protect this delicate ecosystem for future generations. Its preservation is an objective that should be shared by all Australians and endorsed by government at all levels.

The eagerness of our young people on the land: their initiative, innovation and **the great resourcefulness of our youth** is what shapes Queensland for me. It doesn't matter whether the child is a boy or girl, what matters is that the child is determined and has a solid grasp of what he or she wants to do.

Queensland can deliver some harsh climatic conditions, but it is a great place with a sustainable environment for families and business to thrive and grow wherever they may live.

Larry Acton. Enterprising Ways—On Farm. Alexis Hindmarsh feeding the poddy calves at 'Hazeldean', Eidsvold.

Shelly Hindmarsh

**Graham Cumming.** Cane Fire. The last cane fire in the Burdekin for the 2001 cane crushing season at 'Javisfield' via Ayr. 25 October 2001, 5.30pm.

In the Burdekin, centred on Ayr in North Queensland, there are really only two seasons: great summers and perfect winters. The sun shines about 300 days of the year. Unpredictable tropical wet seasons are the only interruption to a year of sunshine. The Burdekin remains one of the few communities in Queensland where from June to November locals and tourists are in awe of the power and heat generated by cane fires with magnificent flames silhouetted against a tropical morning or evening sky. Sugar cane is burnt prior to harvesting. The fires remove the dead thrash from the sugar cane stalks and vermin from the paddock.

Reconciliation is an important goal for all Australians. Museums are making a major contribution to reconciliation by providing a forum where indigenous people can share their stories with the wider community. There has been a substantial shift in the role of a museum from 'expert' to 'facilitator' and a recognition that indigenous knowledge lies with indigenous communities. Monty Pryor wanted his 1962 Garbutt Magpies Captain's trophy to be in the displays at the Museum of Tropical Queensland because he recognised that the museum was an appropriate place to tell his story. Museums must continue to earn this trust and be a positive vehicle for cross-cultural understanding.

Dr Ian Galloway. Monty Pryor with his 1962 Garbutt Magpies Captain's trophy. Garbutt. 14 September 1999.

Ruth Meaglia

Contemporary Queensland culture is richly diverse, readily embracing elements of the new while never forgetting to pay homage to its traditions. This finds expression in 'the shout'. Here a recently arrived South American shares a beer with his Aussie mate against the iconic backdrop of a galvanised iron shed at a bush race meeting in North West Queensland.

Betsy Fysh. The Shout. Carlos Meaglia (left) and Frith Fysh at the McKinlay Races. June 1980.

Tropical heat, hilly terrain, lush vegetation,

houses on stumps, roofs like umbrellas,

rising and falling across the landscape.

Timber and iron, movement and decoration,

heat haze inside, outside filtered light.

Shade: a quiet corner.

# Contemplation, relaxation,

young boys, past and future.

Sunday afternoon on the verandah.

Fiona Gardiner. Sunday afternoon on the verandah. Duncan Hill (age 14) and Fergus Hill (age 12) playing chess. Paddington, Brisbane. 18 November 2001.

# He is a wild and woolly scrubber, my man of thirty years,

His life has been a trial of dust and flies and tears.

He's tough as rawhide rope, as gentle as a lamb,

Through his life he's kept up hope,

My one and only man.

**Marilyn Hughes.** The Man of the West. Gary Hughes—My husband (Glen Hughes in the background) after a hard day's work on the property. 'Dora Park', Meandarra.

No single image can possibly encapsulate a state as diverse as Queensland, but the **major portion of Queensland is cattle country.** This image portrays the essence of the outback—rolling grasslands interspersed with residual hills.

Peter Knowles. Cattle on the Plains. Near Middleton, Western Queensland. 3 April 2001, 9am.

As the sun setting over the Noosa River is gilded by the smoke from the western bushfires, the pelican stalks his last tasty morsel of the day.

The reflected golden shaft of the sun's dying rays guide the kite to its evening resting-place.

The spectacular end to another lazy Noosa Sunday, just as it would have been witnessed for thousands of years by the traditional people of this country.

Only the presence of houseboats at their moorings, awaiting their owner's next pilgrimage to this wonderful paradise, brings this image into contemporary focus.

Cr Bob Abbot. Lazy Noosa Sunday. The Noosaville public boat ramp, Noosa. 15 July 2001, 5.30pm.

Geoff Potter

Chastina Anderson. 'Queenslandah!' Milton Road, Brisbane. May 2001. L to R: Chastina, Henry and Ariane Anderson.

It's an annual ritual—the maroon and blue meeting on the rugby league field. It's a war between the best of the best and a clash where Queensland pride is at stake.

## This pride spans generations, so it was fitting to share my first State of Origin match with my Poppi, Dad and sister.

With generations of others, we walked down the hill past the XXXX brewery to the 'Cauldron'. We were on a mission to ensure that the cane toads won the first match of the 2001 series.

Nothing unites Queensland like State of Origin rugby league.

Black and white in sport we unite…and in reconciliation.

My image of Queensland is one of diversity. Diversity of land and sea, of colours of the waters in and around our reefs and rocky headlands and mangrove forests rich with terrestrial and marine life.

And diversity of people. The richness of individual character adapting to the opportunities and challenges presented by this vast state. From the parched terrains of the south-west corner to the rainforests of the north-east. From the highly populated south-east to the remote shorelines of the Gulf of Carpentaria.

In Queensland we have a great opportunity to achieve sustainable development based on a secure, but still growing, scientific information base. That base must include social, cultural, and economic aspects as well as the ecological. Queensland is well placed to become the 'knowledge resource' of the tropical precincts of the global village. Opportunity knocks.

Dr Joe Baker AO OBE FTSE FRACI. 2001 Queensland Great award winner. Queensland—the Place to Be.

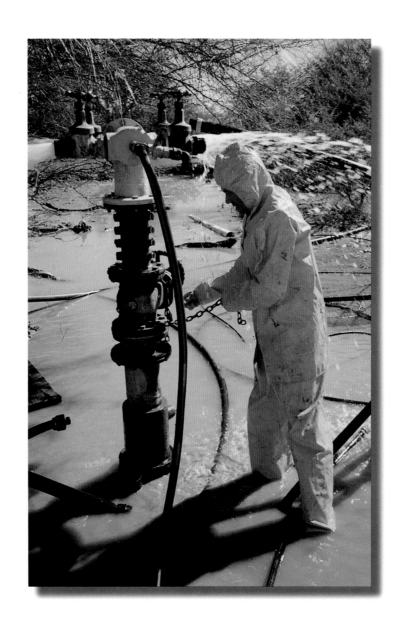

**Elaine Britton.** Workman Colin Britton from the Water Resources replacing headworks on an artesian bore. Rockvale Station, **Julia Creek.** November 1994.

Queensland for me is about the workers who have to travel the outback for weeks at a time to do their job. They, and their families left at home, lead lonely lives with communication often difficult from far-flung areas of the state.

Water Resources employees are an example of these hard workers. Artesian bores were sunk all over the outback to obtain water for stock and often left gushing over the land. These men travelled long distances to place headworks on many bores in an effort to prevent the water from being wasted. The work was often dangerous, with water temperatures reaching boiling point.

Characterised by unique beauty and diversity, with a landscape that has captured the imagination of poets, artists, musicians, and home to me for 55 years, my Queensland is eternally young, brimful of hope and, like a newborn child, open to endless opportunities for growth. To nurture this child fresh from the arms of God, and ensure the future of our buoyant state, each of us must assume responsibility. In this way we can develop a society where education, technology and employment are within reach of all, and dream of a dawn when peace, justice, stability and compassion for the disadvantaged become hallmarks of our Queensland way of life.

Sr Angela Mary Doyle AO RSM. 2001 Queensland Great award winner. Four-day-old Bianca Washington, born ten weeks premature, basks in the warmth of her mother's love. Intensive Care Nursery, Mater Mothers' Hospital, South Bank. 20 November 2001.

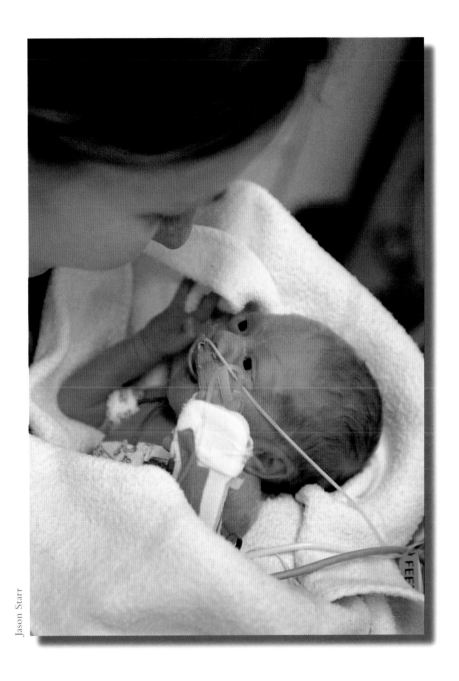

Jason Starr

Sr Angela Mary's vision and determination during her time as the Sister Administrator and Senior Director of Health Services at the Mater Public Hospitals contributed significantly to the development of the Mater Mothers' Hospital's internationally renowned facilities and care for premature and sick newborn babies. Presented by the South Bank Business Association in conjunction with South Bank Corporation.

Joanne Ballard. Sunrise in the Outback. Ilfracombe, Central West Queensland. 4 June 2001, 6.50am.

Daylight sneaking gentle fingers of light through
the crisp morning air—This is my Queensland.

# Beauty unveiled as the day unfolds, pastel hues of pink, mauve and blue, softly filling the outback sky—This is my Queensland.

The strength and might of our glorious sun, slowly
claiming dominance over this vast ancient land—
This is my Queensland.

A hard and often unforgiving place: my heart gently
cradled in her hands—This is my Queensland.

Yesterday I held a dream in my hands.

A dream divinely inspired.

A dream invisible, impossible,

but as real as life to me.


And so I fed a dream in my hands.

As I look into the eyes of those before,

overpowering disbelief of the world.

Thank you, dream maker.


Today I share the dream in my hands.

The dream unseen, to reality.

# The dream that, hands together,

becomes more powerful than death.


And so I see the dream in my hands

as young lives take the dream I shared,

To build into their own.

Thank you, dream maker.


Queensland is a place of dreams … can you see the

dreams in our hands?

Sarah Carter. Dreams in Our Hands. I am a youth worker in Queensland. I encourage countless young people each year to go after and fulfil their dreams. To me, that is contemporary Queensland—growing and releasing people to be all they can be.

H Sydney Curtis. Water Fern. Mount Spec. September 1980.

Queensland: the Sunshine State, blue skies and wide open spaces. But it is the rainforests that are so special and uniquely Queensland. Their exceptional value has been internationally recognised by World Heritage listing. Though comprising less than 0.1 per cent of Australia, the Wet Tropics World Heritage Area has 20 to 60 per cent of the species of each of Australia's plants, birds, butterflies, mammals, reptiles and frogs. The sun shining through a new fern frond represents the many-faceted beauty of Queensland's rainforests and our aspirations for Queensland's future.

As a young boy in the 1930s the Forestry Department told us of native pine. By the mid–1940s most of the native pine was gone. Large amounts of plantation pine was being planted in the Mary Valley, and later on the coastal Wallum land, despite objections by various groups. I have seen these plantations being harvested, and also seen saw mills close and new ones built to handle the volume of pine. The men who oversaw this gigantic task are no longer around to see the results. Without this pine our building industry would be in trouble.

Gordon V Elmer. Mature pine and replant. Looloora Forestry, Rainbow Beach Road, Rainbow Beach. 13 November 2001.

Patricia Cowley. The Last Bale. The loading of wool is completed by family members who also work in the shearing shed. 'Wongalea', Yelarbon. John Cowley and Philip Cowley (in long trousers).

The times for shearing have always been as regular as the seasons in our part of Queensland—early autumn, spring and early summer. As shearing gets underway and the bales of wool start stacking up in the shearing shed, a truck arrives to be loaded and cart the wool to a woolstore to be processed prior to sale. Most shearing sheds cannot hold and store all the bales of wool produced during the shearing period so this procedure is repeated a couple of times. There is always much satisfaction when the last bale is loaded.

Queensland provides me with the opportunity to live **my perfect lifestyle.** In Queensland you can have your cake and eat it too. It's about sunshine, being alive and living. All combined with unlimited opportunity to succeed at any level. I love the place.

Trevor Hendy, Ironman champion. Nippers on Greenmount Beach, Coolangatta.

The wide Barambah Valley and I are 91-year-old friends. My pioneer parents carved a farm out of the scrub almost 100 years ago growing cows, pigs and maize. The valley now grows duboisia (for medical drugs), grapes, olives and macadamia. As I look across the valley, it still speaks to me of its reliable past as it responds to the demands of today and the possibilities for the future. Barambah Valley— reliable, stable, serene and peaceful. Here for posterity.

Bernie Shelton. Boat Mountain Tablelands. Bernie Shelton overlooking Murgon and Wondai Shires. 12 November 2001, 8am.

Its seaways, rivers, lakes and streams.

Its deserts and mountains.

Its flora and fauna, but more, its people,

Aboriginal, Torres Strait Islanders

and all those of many cultures that create the vibrant pulse

that makes us Queensland and Queenslanders.

Dr Robert V Anderson OAM. 2001 Queensland Great award winner. A Ngugi elder from the Quandamooka area, South East Queensland Waters of Moreton Island, Dr Anderson is serving his second term as Chairman of the Aboriginal and Torres Strait Islander Advisory Board. Boronia Rosmarinifolia. Uncle Bob used to collect these flowers when he was a child.

For us and our family, the Sunshine Coast in Queensland is simply 'the best place in the world'.

Grant Kenny OAM and Lisa Curry-Kenny MBE OAM. Mooloolaba Beach, Sunshine Coast.

**Diane Esmond.** Black basalt rocks along the shoreline between Bargara and Innes Park near **Bundaberg.**
11 November 2001, 9.30am.

For me, Queensland's true delight lies in discovering the unexpected. Like this black basalt shoreline near Bundaberg—a little exotic and not the usual Queensland beach. Beaches with long curves of windswept sand to fill a thousand picture postcards are close by, but it's here, where Bundaberg's ancient lava flows tumble black and glistening into the water, that the real magic happens. Just over those rocks, on the submerged lava platforms, grows corals of all shapes and sizes, and colours—Queensland's only on-shore corals. Even the lava rock pools support soft coral growth. Unexpected, isn't it?

Where the whitewood trees are growing

and the bore is softly flowing,

in pastures by the homestead may you rest;

And above your peaceful sleeping,

as we stand in silence, weeping

The evening star shines brightly in the west.


And from the homestead verandah

our eyes, at times, meander

slowly o'er your final resting place;

Where your epitaph cemented is read with

    hearts contented

In dignity you've run and won your race.

Lyn Fraser. 'His' two whitewood trees, just up from the 'Culburnie' Homestead, Barcaldine. 20 October 2001.

Oil painting by Lyn Fraser.

**Louise Donges.** Vic Donges at 'Glenarbon', 40 kilometres north west of Texas on the **Dumaresq River.** March 2001.

Vic Donges is my Granddad. I have placed him in front of the old tobacco hut because both have weathered the years. It also provides a hint of his previous full-time occupation—that of a hard-working farmer. He has lived on this farm for most of his 81 years and from the 1930s to the late 1970s it was a thriving tobacco township. I have such respect for Granddad's generation. They have formed the backbone for future generations. Without their hard work, strength, imagination and experience we would not have evolved into what Queensland is today. I believe this generation truly are the heart and soul of Queensland.

This constantly changing view of the South Burnett wakes me daily. My ancestors challenged freezing temperatures, flash floods and dire droughts, but here I retired to pursue my passion to write, paint and breed the near-extinct taffy horse, prized for its beauty, versatility and intelligence. Now the South Burnett can proudly boast it is home to this restored pony. **I love the welcoming country towns** where whole communities fight fiercely to preserve the South Burnett's original heritage. I am amazed when, following drought, grass grows overnight from one short, sharp shower. Here I feel safe from the fears of our terrorist-stricken world.

Pat Graham. The South Burnett's smile of welcome. South Burnett Highway, Nanango. 3 September 2001, 6.10am.

Sue Gough. A scene from *Paper House*, Interior of La Boite Theatre, Hale Street, Brisbane. 21 August 2001.

Queensland's most thriving cultural community, and the oldest continuously operating theatre company in Australia, Brisbane's La Boite Theatre is the only functioning theatre in the round in Australia. La Boite stages Australian works and aims to encourage debate. When I walk into the foyer it's like coming home. Conversation at interval is a passionate free-for-all. This scene is from *Paper House*, a dramatised account of the lives of refugees who have arrived in Australia over the past 100 years. The production, featuring actors from non-English speaking backgrounds, had much to say to Australians facing the asylum seeker crisis in late 2001.

In 1962 I arrived in Longreach a new bride. The following year torrential rain fell resulting in a flood, which surrounded the town and made the Winton Road impassable for days. This has happened many times over the years and is typical for many of Queensland's remote towns. There had always been talk in government of doing something about these trouble spots. After 37 years money was granted for the **construction of a new road** over the Thomson River. In 7 kilometres, 16 bridges were constructed and many thousands of metres of road materials were carted to the works and compacted down. Now we are waiting anxiously for the next flood, when we will really appreciate the road. It will save many days of lost time for road transport and keep the town accessible for local people and travellers.

Margaret Hislop. Thomson River Bridge.

**June Hansen.** David Parkes from Greening Australia and Estelle Van Kampen with a Mary River Turtle found beside
the **Mary River at Tioro.** Landcare Volunteers were planting trees to provide food and habitat for this endangered species.
9 December 2001.

We've neglected our environment,

to notice we've been slow.

But at last we are enlightened,

we'll show the way to go.

We are stopping banks eroding,

we are making rivers flow.

We are healing mother nature,

# Come on Queensland, Way to Go.

There's koalas in the tree tops,

watching birds nesting below.

With more farms turning organic,

we are reaping what we sow.

And we say to sunny Queensland,

although progress may seem slow,

keep on running with that baton,

Come on Queensland, Way to Go.

The letters in Qantas stand for Queensland and Northern Territory Aerial Services. The air service was conceived in Cloncurry, born in Winton, grew up in Longreach, came of age in Brisbane and reached maturity in Sydney.

Hudson Fysh and Paul McGinness dreamt of operating their own air service under the Southern Cross. Their vision became reality when Qantas was formed on 16 November 1920. With the support of Chairman Fergus McMaster and engineer Arthur Baird, the airline was launched and headed off to link outback towns.

Longreach is proud of its Qantas heritage.

Judy Lasker. The Qantas hangar, the original home to Qantas planes. Longreach. 13 November 2001, 5.45pm.

Trudy Walker

Peter Mylonas

**Ian Fullerton,** second generation Golden Circle pineapple farmer, in a paddock on his property. Ian is wearing traditional garb including protective heavy canvas 'chaps' to prevent scratching from the razor-edged pineapple leaves. Beerwah. 6 December 2001, 11am.

Tropical pineapples ripening in the paddock, the rich, red volcanic soil, the Glasshouse Mountains ever present in the distance, the sun on your skin as you work . . . that's what Queensland is all about to me.

Presented by Golden Circle.

In the evening you can feel the breeze
as it rustles through the waddi trees.
And brings a gentle breath of scented air
that caresses the leaves of trees so rare.
They bow their heads and prey for needed rain
as they struggle to survive on a gibber plain.
The dry arid beauty of this great vast land
is close to the hearts of those who understand.

Carol Anderson. Waddy Wood, Waddi Tree. A rare waddi tree at Montague Downs. August 2000, 4pm.

Reina Irmer. A multicultural group of students at South Bank Institute of TAFE, South Brisbane.
15 November 2001, 12pm.

Growing up in post-war Europe, I witnessed much ethnic, political and social division and intolerance. As a result, I have a deep desire to see people from around the world living together harmoniously.

Since migrating to Queensland in 1983, I have watched Queensland grow, embrace and I have increasingly been proud of the rich diversity of its people. This image, of students attending TAFE in South Brisbane, conveys my contemporary view of Queensland's increased tolerance and acceptance of others. In essence, it displays what it means to be a Queenslander.

Queensland's Performing Arts Centre is the social and cultural hub of Brisbane and northern New South Wales. A diverse cross-section of the community converges in thousands upon this centre all year. They come to be entertained, informed, to observe and absorb all the pleasures it offers.

QPAC, as it is affectionately known, is the jewel in the crown of the nation's performing arts centres.

Peter Lynch. Festive illuminations projected onto the walls of buildings to celebrate the 2001 Goodwill Games, Brisbane. 6 September 2001, 10pm.

Jim Gloriod

For skydivers, Queensland has provided us with the
venue of beautiful blue skies to display our skills.

To be far above the land has shown us a special view.
Here in the sky, Queensland has a dynamic
look: hard to explain, but once viewed, never forgotten.

Come into the sky and then you will know why.

Karen McEvoy. Playing in the sky over Hervey Bay. October 2001.

Peter Boyd

Queensland's unique feature is its contemporary pioneers. They are often self-employed, but are willing to be separated from family and 21st century comforts to endure dust, flies, incredible heat and isolation to deliver a service to the people who live and work in remote parts of the state. Roadworkers have to be totally self-sufficient and usually stay away as long as the fuel lasts which is around 3 to 4 weeks.

Wendy Boyd. Semi and graders. Somewhere between Bedourie and Birdsville. September 1998.

Queensland. A **safe haven** to create what I like.

Gary Crew. Queensland writer. Goodwill Bridge opening **Brisbane,** 21 October 2001, 12.30pm.

This image recalls my 16-day camel ride through this landscape of few horizons, where seasons dominate all life. On our 'Journey across the country', 160 people of mixed age, origin and calling, travelled by camel, horse, wagon, Cobb & Co coach or on foot, camping along the route blazed by **the pioneers we sought to honour.** Like them we endured frosts, rain, winds and heat, but camaraderie grew and dry Queensland humour helped. Around our final campfire, I relished how trekkers' own songs and verses revealed their pride in this unique adventure and echoed my fascination with the real Queensland in 2001.

Joan Heatley. Queensland Government Stock Route near Middleton in Central Western Queensland.
Part of a cavalcade marking more than 70 years of service by Cobb & Co, whose skills with horses and camels once linked Queensland's isolated western pioneers to the distant coastal settlements they had left behind. 10 July 2001.

Pauline Cox

Steve Hutchins. My son, David enjoying his new pool in the backyard. Aspley, Brisbane. Christmas 1999.

I love the pure joy of this shot. What could be better,
**playing in the water in your
own backyard** on a perfect Queensland
summer day. He has heroes—go Thorpie, go Lleyton,
go Pat, go 'Wobbalies' (Wallabies), go Broncos. It doesn't
matter whether they win or lose. Free from the shadow
of terrorism, global warming, unemployment. No
confusion about whether he is sorry. It is a shame
that this will change.

Aboriginal people have strong religious beliefs. We are also rich in spirituality, ceremonies, legends and lore. The religious side gives us self-assurance and assertiveness without being self-centred.

No matter how large our problems, we have always managed to find the strength to endure all complexities. There is the old way and a new way. If the two ways do not come together we are not acting right towards each other.

# We must come together as Australians, each of us unique in our own special way. Each of us not forgetting where we are from, and never losing sight of where we are going.

Margaret Iselin. The signing of the Native Title process agreement between the Quandamooka Land Council Aboriginal Corporation and the Redland Shire Council. It shows Minjerribah-Moorgumpin Elder Aunty Margaret Iselin and Redland Mayor Eddie Santagiuliana. North Stradbroke Island. August 1997.

**Kevin Kerr.** An Image in Time. A sign on a bush gate on a track which leads to the waterholes on the Diamantina River known as 'The Gates' between Diamantina Lakes Homestead and Brighton Downs Homestead, part of the Diamantina National Park. 19 July 1996.

*Now faith is the substance of things hoped for, the evidence of things not seen.*

*Hebrews, c11, v1*

Faith in God, who created this land, and a tribute to the faith and hopes of those who explored, surveyed and settled in this harsh environment and to those who presently manage it.

In times of flood the channels of the Diamantina River break their banks and waters rise to above the fence level.

When the floods recede—The Promised Land: green grass, flowers, thousands of birds, fish in abundance and grazing pastures to fatten cattle for domestic and international markets.

As sure as He feeds the birds, He feeds us.

Alone through the night he stumbled,

along the dirt-paved street,

searching for somewhere to sleep,

a place to rest his feet.


# Guided by the soft yellow glow,

he stumbled in the door,

on the wooden floors of the hotel,

he rested his weary soul.


Now on those same floorboards they dance,

to the music in their hearts,

twisting, weaving, stamping, singing,

their time has just begun.


Below them on high stools they perch,

men whose time has gone,

with the clink of glasses, the hum of voices,

they conjure up the past.


Elise Jamieson. Established in 1893, the Queens Hotel has undergone many renovations and facelifts over the years, the most recent in 2001. It is representative of many places throughout Queensland where historic buildings are still being used today. Ayr. 18 November 2001, 1.30pm.

**Milynda Heaton-Rogers.** Clancie and Faith Rogers have just completed an on-air preschool lesson with the Longreach School of Distance Education. The schoolroom at **Boongoondoo Station, Jericho.** 9 November 2001, 12.30pm.

Queensland's greatest resource is its children. Educating them, encouraging vitality, determination and community spirit are very important. Wonderful things are never accomplished without enthusiasm and Queenslanders have that in abundance. We must continue to **instil self-confidence and motivation in our youth** so that they are ready for the opportunities that arrive. Wherever our children reside—the isolated outback, the coast or in the city—they need our encouragement to help them be the best that they can be. Because Queensland is the state of opportunities.

Frogs lead a chorus, wallabies graze.
King browns bask in the clearing.
Lizards laze, dingo hunts—
for eleven months.

Bandicoot digs, possum scents blossom.
Fruit bats swarm to their food source in thousands,
traversing the pink evening skies—
for eleven months.

Visitors cluster for Gympie Muster.
Musicians gravitate eagerly;
thousands of faces, drawn to return.
Trees reverberate. Country music
replaces the bellbirds' delicate peals—briefly.

As wallabies repossess, rats sniff the air,
dismissing odd human behaviour.
Scrub turkeys scuffle, frogs sing unchallenged—
for eleven months.

Lorne Maitland. Forest Entertainer. Bedecked by native trees, the Country Music Muster site is in the care of mother nature most of the year. Queensland State Forest, Amamoor. 12 February 2002, 8am.

Dennis Wilson

Glen Threlfo

Catherine O'Reilly. Antarctic beech trees—thousands of years old—wonders of nature. Lamington National Park.

If we could retain something of the child within us
and share with these boys the magic of
ancient trees.
To explore with them the caves of their gnarled roots
exposed by the erosion of a thousand years.
To respect the heritage that is ours,
to revere it and care for it
and pass it on to children of distant generations
with pride in our vision of Queensland.

# The Tree of Knowledge in Barcaldine holds special significance in Queensland's history. The meeting site during the Great Shearers' Strike of 1891, it became the birthplace of the Australian Labor Party. In July 2001, 110 years later, the Queensland Biennial Festival of Music chose the tree as a meeting place for artists from across the world to launch the opening of this special celebration. Over 10 days the magic of music connected communities throughout Queensland. As we develop our 'Smart State' let's also celebrate our history, and Queensland—like our famous tree—will continue to strengthen and grow.

Colleen Horn. The Barcaldine Big Marimba Band joined by Dutch percussion ensemble Anumadutchi in an inspiring performance under the Tree of Knowledge at the opening of the Queensland Biennial Festival of Music. Barcaldine. 20 July 2001.

Greg Horn

Peter Hosking

Anne McMurray. Serenity. Burleigh Heads beach looking north. 14 August 2000, 5.15pm.

Queensland

# A golden coast

health

and wellbeing shaped

and moulded

by the landscape. Young

and old rejuvenated in the receding tide,

capturing, for each day,

a personal

shiny

moment.

Queensland's schools are highly diverse and dynamic communities. The Kalki Out-station in beautiful Cape York is an example of the school going to the students. The teachers use small motor boats to transport themselves, curriculum materials and camping equipment to this remote site outside Aurukun. The 21 children arrived at the river bank site by 'school bus', a tractor. These talented children are tri-lingual and use their Aboriginal language, Kriol and English to learn. The school sessions occur monthly in intensive blocks of time. Queensland has always come up with many ingenious ways of responding to its remote populations and the Kalki Out-station is one good example of this responsiveness.

Marilyn McMeniman. A Queensland Government review team visits the Kalki Out-station during the Queensland Government's review of the Queensland school curriculum (Shaping the Future) in 1993.

Lyle Radford

Cr Paul Pisasale. Bendigo Bank building, corner of Limestone and East Streets, Ipswich. January 2002.

This classic Bendigo Bank Queensland heritage building in Ipswich is meticulously preserved, centrally positioned and innovatively utilised. Queensland's heritage city of Ipswich is building a sustainable future while preserving the past. The historic bank building embodies the philosophy of contemporary Queensland, to preserve the past for the betterment of tomorrow.

The Bendigo Bank has a proud and successful partnership with the city of Ipswich, which is the oldest provincial city in Queensland. It is showing a strong leadership role in heritage preservation, community banks, youth development and community telco. Ipswich is proud of its past, excited about its future and boldly markets the city as a great place.

University of Queensland research students at Heron Island on Queensland's Great Barrier Reef. Arguably the **best protected reef** in the world, the Great Barrier Reef is an Australian national icon. By developing a better understanding of this intricate tropical environment and the effects of global warming, researchers believe they can assist in the management of reefs around the world.

University of Queensland PhD students in the Centre for Marine Studies, Anke Kluter (L) and Angela Lawton collecting samples on the reef off UQ's Heron Island Research Station. 28 February 2001.

David Sproule

Presented by The University of Queensland.

Rob Butler

**Sarah Kirk.** Looking Forward. Genevieve Dunn resting on part of a sculpture in the Brolga Theatre's surrounds. **Maryborough.** 15 November 2001, 6.30am.

A world of opportunity is in the hands of the youth of Maryborough. Built on strong industrial foundations, Maryborough has been supported by flourishing timber, sugar and engineering industries since its earliest settlement. This stable foundation, coupled with the foresight, generosity and enthusiasm of community leaders, has enabled the provision of wonderful sporting, cultural, educational and recreational opportunities and created a true spirit of community. Growing up in regional Queensland is a treasure. With stability at our backs and opportunities at our feet, the future for Maryborough's youth can only be bright.

Peter Lik

My Queensland oozes an attitude of fresh optimism with **character and colours of crystalline quality.** Those privileged enough to call Queensland home enjoy a lifestyle of unparalleled wealth, where the best things in life are free.

Alex de Waal. A pristine beach with crystal clear water, Lizard Island. 14 July 2000, 11am.

Stewart Gould

The Energex Community Rescue Helicopter is
one of four community helicopter rescue services
partly financed by the Queensland Government.
One of the aims of the service is to provide rapid
emergency medical services to
rural and remote areas of Queensland.

Hayden Kenny. The Energex Community Rescue Helicopter at the Helicopter Rescue base, Sunshine Coast Airport,
Marcoola. 1 November 2001.

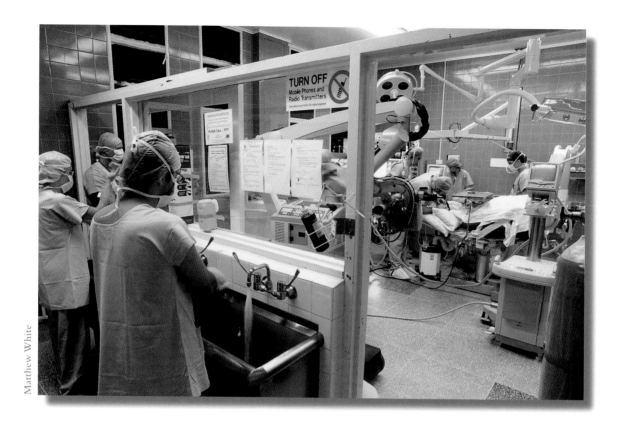

Matthew White

Queensland: It's not only the weather that's bright.

Dr Scott F Campbell. Preparation for Spinal Surgery. The neurosurgical team at the Royal Brisbane Hospital Neurosurgical Operating Theatre. 13 November 2001, 10am.

Because of my love of the outdoors and fishing, I would have to say Moreton Bay is so special at first light, in my father-in-law's boat, fresh bait and a couple of crab pots.

# A feed of fish, sand crabs and an ice cold beer when you get back. Sounds like Queensland to me—you gotta love it!

Troy Cassar-Daley. Country music singer. Golden Beach, Caloundra.

Queensland is where I choose to make my home. As a photographer, I revel in its warm and sensuous beauty. As a publisher, I depend on its commercial efficiency and technological nous.

From Brisbane, I look to nature for spiritual nourishment and find an embarrassment of riches within reach. Dawn is, to me, a magic time of day **best experienced beside the ocean's vastness.** My senses record the breeze through the pandanus, the rolling surf and the salty air, and I carry this in my imagination forever, even in the heart of the desert.

Steve Parish. Photographer. Stradbroke Dawning. Sunrise over the Pacific, shot through pandanus, Frenchmans Beach, North Stradbroke Island. 9 March 2001.

Dr Sally-Ann Poulsen. Captivation in the Queensland Backyard. Aramara North. April 1988.

A cane toad that has found itself a cosy but temporary home in a hole dug for a clothesline captivates my nieces and nephews Peita, Michelle and Neil Ward-Pearson and James, William and David Bargenquast. This candid image demonstrates the joy and fascination of children with the wonders found in most every Queensland backyard. Queensland children are privileged in having pleasant weather year round. Much of their childhood can be spent exploring the fascinations that outdoor living provides, setting them apart from many children elsewhere in Australia and the rest of the world.

The gallantry of those who represented their communities in times of conflict, greatly contributed to the wealth and status of Queensland. They added to the mix of the wonderful resources that make living in the Sunshine State a symbol of an ideal lifestyle.

# The sensitive gesture of laying a wreath responds to that need to remember and respect those who contributed to our existing wealth. Upholding the tradition of Anzac Day continues to enhance the spirit of Queensland communities, as people from all generations contribute and respond.

Diane Merchant. Returning to Remember. The wreath-laying ceremony, Anzac Day, Barcaldine. 25 April 2000, late morning.

David Mayocchi

Mary-Rose MacColl. South-east Queensland Rainforest. May 2001, early morning.

In Brisbane, Harriet was learning, wild things grew uncontrollably because of the sun which was without modesty. New estates might carve into the hills, but Harriet had started to see that the whole place was **underpinned by a forest** that would overwhelm everything if the people left for a decade or so and let the summers do their work. 'Our most livable city,' the signs from the airport said. 'But livable for what?' Harriet had asked a taxi driver the week before. He'd fallen silent. She'd assumed he was reflecting on the idea.

Extract from *Angels in the Architecture*

My Queensland is about the camaraderie of the stockmen around Boulia where I worked for 6 years. All year round, ringers from neighbouring stations would attend the cattle muster, helping out and making the job a lot easier. There was also a fair amount of rivalry. Fortunately there was never grog in the camp or the axe lying on the ground would have been lethal.

The ex-army Ford Blitz lorry (pictured) was the chuckwagon. It carried everything from tucker to swags, drinking water, supplementary horse feed and cooking gear. The old Blitz was handy in sandy country with its aircraft-type balloon tyres. Often the self-starter failed on the V8 engine and the trusty old crank handle had to be put to use.

Almost 40 years on, I am fortunate enough to occasionally load up the 4WD equipped with portable fridge, gas barbeque, grog and fillet steak to return to 'Dreamtime'.

Tony (Ned) Rivas. Dinner Camp. An almost dry waterhole on the south-east corner of Springvale Station, about 200 kilometres from Boulia. L to R: J McDonald, R Oates, G Fitzerald, R Donnellan, G Fisher, L Lewis, T McDonald, K Issacson. September 1965, 7.30pm.

Glenda McKnight

**Irene Ryder.** Irene Ryder stands beneath the Foster family's pepperina tree at 'Yumba', Mitchell. 10 November 2001, around midday.

The pepperina tree is a landmark for my family, the Fosters, at Yumba.

Many Aboriginal people lived at Yumba until the council bulldozed it. Some people were taken away and died of a broken heart because they wouldn't come home. When we had a reunion, people came from all over Australia to reminisce about Yumba. We pay respect to the Elders of the Land.

The children are saying, 'This is our land, Yumba'. I share with the schoolchildren the story of how we lived there.

Now the council and Aborigines are working together.

Country music's echoing across the forest floor

as 60,000 visitors flock to Amamoor.

They're junkies for the atmosphere:

# great music, great mates, the occasional beer,

but it's our Queensland spirit that really brings them here.


For this great Aussie celebration happens every year

because of a host of community groups and many a

volunteer, working together tirelessly to lend a helping

hand to raise funds for charities to help those on the land.

This is what it's all about—the spirit of Queensland.


So look out every August—the Aussies are out to have fun.

The forest comes alive—the roos are on the run.

We've got some serious fundraising and playing up to do

at this spectacular event, that's magic through and through.

The Muster, proudly Queensland in spirit—tried and true.


Brian Sansom. Muster Magic. The Toyota National Country Music Muster is Australia's largest outdoor country music event. The Main Stage, Muster site, Amamoor Creek State Forest Park, Amamoor. 26 August 2000, 10pm.

Mark Straker

Diane Cilento. 2001 Queensland Great award winner. Delini McPherson on the veranda at 'Karuak'.

I love verandah living,

hammock and drying line.

Brown bare feet, and lovely heat,

that's Queensland all the time.

# I love verandah living,

the roar of rain on iron.

Discarded thongs, and cane toad songs,

that's Queensland and it's mine.

Roger Llott

Here is an image of the Queensland I love, where we celebrate modern technological achievement together with an artistic reminder of the pioneers of the past.

Carved on the naturally occurring granite boulders overlooking the dam are these magnificent sculptures of Patrick Leslie and his wife Kate, the earliest European pioneers of the district, keeping watch over the dam named in their honour. They are the work of Leyburn sculptor, Vernon Foss.

Bill Scott. Leslie Dam, Darling Downs. 20 November 2001, 9.15am.

The Australian Workers Heritage Centre allows visitors to experience the hardships and victories of the workers who helped shape the quality of life and working conditions Queenslanders (and Australians) have today. Its location marks the spot of Australia's first major industrial dispute: the Great Shearer's Strike of 1891.

Eileen Haueuschild-Tourell. Out of the past. Burnsie's Billabong and the Bicentennial Theatre. A small part of the Australian Workers Heritage Centre, Barcaldine.

Alastair Bett

Queensland acknowledges cultural diversity and provides endless opportunities. It offers a **relaxed lifestyle** and there is nothing better than going to the beach for a swim.

I wouldn't swap it for the world.

Vicki Wilson OAM. Former Australian netball captain. South Bank, Brisbane. 26 January 2002, 1.10pm.

Kate Shapcott

In the adult years,

we didn't need the obvious river.

But it was always just beyond the paddocks

or over the rise, flowing casually

and with its own momentum.

Once you are aware of the river

as a live movement you know the pulse

and it outpaces your own breath

although, like breath, it promises certainty.

Tom Shapcott. Quart Pot Creek in flood. January 2001, 8am.

Peter Curtain

Bernie Carroll. At 'Old Boyneside'. Visitors from the city are amazed and entranced by Tom Curtain and his working dogs who follow his every command. 12 November 2000.

Having lived at 'Old Boyneside' all my life, it has always been my own special part of Queensland. A life on the land brings the contrasts of great enjoyment from the bounty of a good season to the despair of drought and financial hardship. It is with great satisfaction that I see young people of our next generation have a willingness and courage to **accept the enormous challenges of rural life,** are innovative and confident enough to grasp the opportunities and yet maintain a deep love and care for the land itself.

One of my favourite things about the Gold Coast is its sense of fun. The Coast is synonymous with leisure, with a vibrant culture of nightlife and entertainment. The cabaret and club scenes of the 1960s and 1970s were exhilarating. I have wonderful memories of early beach entertainment venues like the Play Room (which Claude Carnell and later myself operated for the next two decades), the Skyline, Cabbage Patch, Broadie, Jet Club, Grand and Coolangatta Hotels. I have enjoyed the changing fashions in popular types of live music, song and dance such as cabaret, discos and rock. Entertainment venues have changed, but I still sense the fun and excitement that emerges after every sunset at the many diverse nightspots throughout the Gold Coast.

Beryl Carnell. It's Hot in Brisbane but it's Cool'n'gatta. New Zealand band Split Enz with internationally acclaimed brothers Neil and Tim Finn. Gold Coast. 1978.

**R Downes.** Hometown Heroes. L to R: Martin Love, Matt Hayden and Katrina Downes with the Sheffield Shield.
**Kingaroy** Cricket and Sports Club. 15 December 1995.

Martin Love from Mundubbera and Matthew Hayden from Kingaroy are two contemporary Queensland cricketers. They were among the young blood in the Queensland team which won the Sheffield Shield in 1995, the first time Queensland had won the Shield since its entry into the competition in 1926. These young players were, and still are, heroes in their home towns.

The Empire Theatre, built in 1911, catered for touring theatrical productions and local concerts. Destroyed by fire in 1933, it was rebuilt in 1935 to operate as a cinema with some touring shows. It closed in 1970 with the screening of *South Pacific*. The Empire was used as a TAFE College for some years prior to being acquired by the Toowoomba City Council in 1993, to restore and operate as a professional regional theatre.

It opened in 1997 as the largest regional theatre in Australia, seating 1,567 people. It is the only restored live theatre in Queensland. The Empire Theatre has served the cultural needs of the Darling Downs for eighty years and is now equipped to serve the area into the future.

Dorothy Singe. The Empire Theatre. A cultural icon of Toowoomba and region.

Dr Pat Dale. Nudgee Beach. 5 November 2001, 5:45pm.

I've lived in Queensland for over 30 years and as part of my research at Griffith University have spent many hours among the mangroves, on the mudflats and enjoying inter-tidal environments. These places are special as they're on the interface between land and sea and support a rich variety of specialised resident animals and plants as well as birds and fish which visit as the tides change. But they're also threatened places, affected directly by human encroachment and indirectly by climate changes. Despite this, I believe they will endure as sustainability becomes an increasing priority among decision-makers.

Presented by Griffith University.

# Fraser Island: wild, beautiful, ancient, unique.

A World Heritage wonder and the largest sand island in the world, towering rainforest grows in sand next to crystal clear freshwater lakes and endless pristine beaches. It is nature's theme park—a paradise full of natural attractions.

Fraser Island's history mirrors that of Queensland, from its rich, ancient indigenous past to its once dominant primary industries of forest logging and sand mining to today, where tourism represents Fraser Island and the region's economic future.

Gary Smith. Fraser Island—a Moment in Time. An ancient rainforest tree has been covered by the sands of Stonetool Sand Blow and then exposed after hundreds of years as the sand moves on. Stonetool Sand Blow, east coast of Fraser Island. March 2001, 4.30pm.

Peter Meyer

**Dianne Thorley.** Friends picnicking in the park reflect the sense of community. The trees surrounding them, some more than 150 years old, give a sense of permanence and security. Queen's Park, Toowoomba. 14 August 2001, around midday.

Toowoomba is unlike any other place in Queensland. The people who settled here came predominantly from the land and we still have that practical, innovative and friendly philosophy that makes this city so different from those on the coastal strip.

Toowoomba people have time to stop and talk no matter how busy their lives. They are people who **easily form that community spirit** that other cities work so hard to capture. This is a place where the quality of life we now have stemmed from foresight in the 19th century. Big shady trees, open parks and wide streets make any part of Toowoomba a wonderful place to live.

This city is the thinking person's paradise.

When flying home to Cairns, I eagerly peer out, seeking the familiar coral cays whose vivid colours look like vast Australian opals from the air. When the plane flies over land, the agricultural fields appear as a work of art made of velvets, corduroys and velours. Driving north from Cairns to my mountain home in the Kuranda rainforest, within earshot of the Barron Falls, I sometimes glimpse this typical cane farm with its **corduroy ploughed field ready for planting.** In the cycle of the seasons, this is usually hidden behind the tall feather-top flowering cane awaiting harvest.

Eve Stafford. Cane farm off the Captain Cook Highway north of Cairns. Spring 2000, early morning.

Robert Silman

Rowena Trieve. The South Sea Islander Canecutter Memorial, South Sea Islander Lagoons Meeting House, Mackay. L to R: Councillor Julie Boyd, Mayor of Mackay; La Paani Boah, Eton State Primary School student; Rowena Trieve, Australian South Sea Islander Elder.

Contemporary Queensland is a mixture of the old and the new. I reflect on the past and where I've come from and then I look forward and new horizons beckon. I think what does the future hold for me and my people?

Sometimes the mists of despair have clouded our visions. Then recognition and acceptance came after years of uncertainty and lingering in the shadows. We've stepped into the sunlight to a brighter future with many golden opportunities.

How proud I am to be a Queensland-born Australian South Sea Islander.

Proud of our past, talented, inventive and aware of our place in the world today, embracing the future with confidence and flair and passing on to our children an understanding and acceptance of global cultures.

Contemporary Queensland is encapsulated by the 'Strictly Boonah' street festival, staged by about 400 community volunteers in the country town of Boonah.

This image incorporates the classic, century-old Queensland county pub (a symbol of our past), the ingenuity and talent of a small rural community in touch with the world (our present) and the initiative and flair of our younger generation (our future).

Dany Weus. Art Smart. The 'Strictly Boonah' street festival. Boonah. 27 October 2001, 7pm.

Queensland to me is epitomised by the lifestyle we enjoy. The beautiful weather, endless beaches, outdoor lifestyle and that **laid back attitude to life** is what lets me know that I'm home in Queensland.

Pat Rafter. Australian of the Year 2002. Whitehaven Beach in the Whitsundays.

We have wide open spaces where I can do the things I like, especially riding camels, horses and my motorbike.

My backyard is 300 square kilometres and it gives me room to do anything. I feel safe and happy here. Queensland has the best weather. Even though it gets very hot here I wouldn't like to live anywhere else.

Tom Woodhouse (age 10). Camels on their first trek at Boulia Rodeo and Race Grounds. Boulia. August 1997.

As a migrant, you never know what's in store for you
when you arrive. To be accepted into the community is
part of a migrant's dream. The awarding of an Order of
Australia medal for my welfare education and training
and teaching was the culmination of a long-fought
battle of acceptance and integration
—one of the ideals of contemporary Queensland.

Dympna Kimmorley OAM JP. Government House. L to R: Norman Kimmorley, Dympna Kimmorley, Her Excellency the
Governor of Queensland Leneen Ford AC and Zani Carter. Brisbane. 22 September 1995, 11am.

At its best, contemporary Queensland is full of possibilities and keeps getting better at taking those possibilities out to the world and doing great things with them.

Nick Earls is the author of seven books and was a finalist in the Queensland Premier's Export Award in 1999.
The Brisbane skyline bathed in the late afternoon sun.

Robby Nason

Bryan Nason AM. On the banks of the Condamine at 'Newington', Surat. 1999.

However new the world,

however violent and turbulent our human action in it,

however strong are our hopes that it might yet

   become better,

however brave and new and vast the world,

nonetheless where we are standing at any moment

   is still somehow the centre.

# This great coolibah tree, ancient

   and stately,

on the black soil plain of the big river at Surat,

is for me and my brother and my sisters

a soul-nourishing image stretching from long

   distant childhood

right up to the moment of today's sunrise.

You won't find my heroes in comic books
You'll find them on the beach.

My heroes don't wear masks or capes
They wear red and yellow caps.

My heroes don't fight for truth and justice
They battle the wind and the waves.

My heroes aren't the kind that save the world
But they did save my life.

Brett Williamson. Heroes. Luke Ingwersen, Queensland Surf Lifesaver. Northcliffe Beach, Gold Coast. 20 March 2001, 8am.

Dean Saffron

153

Leanne Thompson Wilson. The Power of Stories. May 2001.

Queensland is a state with a challenging history but is it also a contemporary state that acknowledges the past and celebrates today and the future. It is rich in cultural diversity, unique places and many stories, some already told and some yet to be shared.

This sacred site called 'The Palace' is where many stories have been handed down. I am a descendant of the Bidjara and Kara-Kara nations and I am sharing the dreaming stories and responsibilities with my youngest son Bayley. I teach him about the artwork and spiritual aspects of The Palace. The old people who now journey with us in spirit wanted The Palace to be a place of sharing and healing, a learning centre where children and their families gather, listen and learn about an ancient culture that continues to survive today.

On arriving we know about the differences, but in the sharing we experience the sameness.

It's not all glitz and glamour at the Gold Coast. Not far from the Palazzo Versace and the ritzy cafes of Tedder Avenue, sometimes in the shadows of the high-rises, you come across the remnants of other eras. Home now to itinerants, students, pensioners and the casualised workers of the tourist industry. I don't remember the exact location of these 'units'. Maybe they've been demolished and replaced by 'luxury townhouses' or yet another high-rise. But despite creeping gentrification and the rush to gated, high-security suburban enclaves, older more open Gold Coast communities like Southport and Labrador are maintaining a vibrant mix of people and housing styles.

Grahame Griffin. Unit to Let. Southport, Gold Coast. May 1996, 4pm.

Ross Woodrow

Ingrid Woodrow. Glisten. Ingrid Woodrow, aged 4, and her mother Jocelyn Woodrow on the verandah of their house.
Mount Morgan. October 1975.

It's me and my Mum.

This is how it use to be:

My Queensland.

We are on the verandah of our house in Mount
    Morgan;

the blush still on my cheeks from running around
    down near the river,

playing in the Lantana. There's my dog
    Alligator—he died.

There's the cane chair—

Mum loved it passionately. Its rain-drenched,
    sun-bleached, mildewed arm.

I threw it onto a trailer-load to be taken to the dump
    the other day.

And there she is.

My boyfriend says: 'Those lips!'

And her eyes:

I can see my father, glistening in the blue.

An extremely small place 500ks or so

west of the big smoke—not how the crow goes,

Is my view of Queensland: the place I call home.


Each year my highlight is to travel to the place I love best

to Mum and Dad's home all trimmed like the rest.

With gorgeous Christmas lights to everyone's delight.


A Christmas at Wallumbilla is like
    no other

with my brother, sisters, father and mother.

Extended families, our grandmothers,

my new partner and son

Quite a special time to spend with everyone.


Tammy Houston. Lights of Home. Christmas lights at 'Wallumbilla'. December 2000.

Ian Houston

Lynelle Urguhart

**Jemma Urguhart.** Pigs in Mud. L to R: Jemma (age 7) and Amy Urguhart (age 4). 'Warrowa', **Moonie.** Mid-October, 1999, about 4pm.

One hot October afternoon a big thunderstorm blew in. It rained heavily for a while, then the power went out like it usually does when there's lightning about.

After the storm, we played in the puddles. It was fantabulous. We used the kickboard to 'surf' down the slope into a big puddle and had mud fights for ages.

When we went to wash the mud off we had no water because the power was still off. We got into a big drum of water outside to wash.

My image of Queensland is taken from my experience of the changing beauty of the east coast as I travelled from Brisbane to Cairns on the 'Sunlander' train. It began with boarding at Roma Street station where, after dispersing of luggage, passengers scurry along with rugs and pillows looking for their carriage to settle in. After leaving the station I watch **the changing scenery** from suburban backyards, markets and parks to the countryside with cattle, goats and even a camel farm. Further north the olive trees, mangoes and banana groves appear. The trees begin to change and become rainforest and as we travel through the far north, acres and acres of sugar cane appear. As we arrive in Cairns, I am amazed at the diversity our state has to offer.

Edith Edwards. Overlooking sugar cane farms near Cairns. December.

Bill Kerr. Burdekin cane grower Paul Sgarbossa in his cane fields checking for cane beetles.
Home Hill, North Queensland. October 1999.

North Queensland cane grower Paul Sgarbossa typifies the fighting spirit and determination of the 6,500 cane-growing families and Queenslanders in general. They are the foundation stones for an industry which is one of the world's largest exporters of raw sugar—the state's most valuable farm crop. Paul's parents began supplying cane to Inkerman Mill at Home Hill in the early 1940s. He and his wife Judith now grow over 12,000 tonnes of cane on the banks of the Burdekin River.

A place of serenity and contemplation, a touch of paradise can now be found just a few short steps away from the Ipswich CBD. Nerima Japanese Gardens at Queens Park is evidence of all that is good about Ipswich's harmonious and growing relationship with our global partners.

This authentic Japanese-style garden adjoins a nature centre portraying all things Australian. Dedicated volunteers painstakingly oversee both the gardens and the nature centre for the enjoyment of all age groups.

Nerima Gardens, Burleigh Griffin Drive, Queens Park, Ipswich.

Presented by Ipswich City Council.

Coominya, from the Aboriginal name Kung-I-Nya meaning 'I see water', nestles between Lake Wivenhoe and Lake Atkinson, 80 kilometres west of Brisbane. It is home to the historic Bellevue Homestead and about 1,000 Queenslanders.

The town has retained its **turn-of-the-century character** boasting a general store and newsagent, pub, public hall, post office and a school.

Syd Linde. Coominya Railway Station, once part of historic Bellevue Homestead.

Music teaching and freelance composing could have
taken me to any number of places around Australia,
but it was always difficult to consider leaving my home
town of Kingaroy not to mention a state as
beautiful as Queensland. So it was here that
my wife and I settled down. Is it any surprise that
we would want our children to grow up here as well?

Russell Bauer. Relaxing. Jessica (L) and Sarah Bauer, O'Neill Square with peanut silos in the background, Kingaroy.
19 November 2001, 5pm.

A magical moment when the brilliant summer solstice
light pierces the cool darkness of
the limestone cave. The sun passes over a shaft in the
Belfry Cavern and beams of dazzling sunlight enter the
dark cave illuminating the roof and walls. The unique
natural phenomenon encapsulates the wondrous blend
of sunshine on an ancient landscape of great natural
beauty. This electrifying experience represents the
essence of Queensland.

Ann Augusteyn. The Summer Solstice Spectacle. Capricorn Caves, Rockhampton. 22 December 2000, 12 noon.

Queensland thrives on its services, on which our quality of life in the community depends. In isolated, rural Queensland, responsive leadership and community teamwork save lives. Queensland is about **performing well in the face of adversity.** All Queenslanders foster the spirit of mateship, which Australians are known for, and it is this spirit that creates the individual characters that can be found in every country town and city.

Cameron Castles. Spirit of Mateship. The Department of Emergency Services on the Diamantina Development Road, Cooladdi.

Jackie Huggins. The sandstone walls of Carnarvon Gorge National Park.

My soul and being are rooted in this place—my home called Queensland. As a proud Murrie woman I am a member of one of the longest surviving cultures on the planet. Way before Federation was decreed my heritage spanned this land. I can proudly boast that I am 2,500th generation Queenslander.

I adore my homeland despite the hardships of the past and present and what has occurred throughout our sad history. But there is hope and I am optimistic that one day reconciliation will reign supremely in our country and that Queenslanders will lead the way.

190,000 years old and 160 kilometres long, the Undara Lava Tubes in the Undara Volcanic National Park were created by the longest lava flow from a single volcano on our planet and can be seen from the moon. Located south-west of Cairns, custodian Gerry Collins once owned the Lava Tubes as part of his grazing property. In 1987 he and his family decided the best way to share these dramatic, ancient formations and protect them for future generations was to develop a **sustainable visitor experience.** They proposed a national park be gazetted around the caves. Gerry's actions reflect the quintessential values of today's Queensland outback. Talk little, do much, walk softly, share freely.

Helen Simpson. Visitors, including world-renowned naturalist David Attenborough, listen as Gerry Collins shares his intimate knowledge of the Undara Lava Tubes in the Undara Volcanic National Park. October 1991.

Scott Hocknull, Young Australian of the Year 2002. South of Winton, central-east Queensland.

The past is our key to the future. Looking down on this ancient Queensland landscape, seemingly devoid of life, we see the history of this region locked away in rocks almost 100 million years old. It tells a story of a time when expansive forests, lakes and streams, teaming with life covered our interior—a time when giant dinosaurs wandered the outback. These giants' fossilised bones are now strewn across our dry, desolate interior and tiny lizards use their bones as perfect sunny spots. Our environment is forever changing and can't be controlled. As a species, we need to listen to the record in the rock and use this as the template for our future.

The past has played an important role in contemporary Queensland. In 1985 a group of dedicated Gympie citizens had a dream to restore the derelict Queensland **Railway Engine No 45.** It was restored to its former glory in 1998 and is now a major tourist attraction for Gympie and district. It has carried over 40,000 passengers since its restoration and rejuvenated the small communities around it.

David Nimmo. The Valley Rattler. Queensland Railway Engine No 45. Gympie.

Chris Lee

Kristy Hinze. International model, courtesy Vivien's Model Management Australia. Roma Street Parklands, Brisbane. 7 April 2001, 11am.

Queensland, the place I call home
and though many places and countries I roam,
I long for the day when I can be there
with blue skies above and clean fresh air.

My childhood memories of just being me,
riding my horses or with friends by the sea,
are so very different to the life I lead now
though I'm **always drawn back**
to Queensland somehow.

With places to travel and people to see,
there is still no place like home
and that's Queensland for me.

As we live in one of the fastest growing coastal destinations in Australia, our local community and government are conscious of the fact that we have to develop and grow sensibly and not to the detriment of our natural attractions. In the background is Ross Creek which consists of a bat colony in mangrove habitat and a safe haven for recreational boats. The Osprey Nest is on the power pole.

This image captures our Capricorn Coast character, the heart and soul of Queensland being our respect for living in harmony with our unique natural attractions. Our tourism is equally about natural as well as man-made attractions, ensuring a balance of protection and progress.

Mary Carroll. We Live Here Too. The Scenic Highway, Ross Street, Yeppoon. 13 November 2001, 12 noon.

Des Byers. Looking Back. Cows after noon milking wandering past the old Moregatta school yard. Moregatta Road, Millaa Millaa.

There's an old school yard at Moregatta
where now no pupil ever goes,
by a creek they call Theresa,
a few miles west of Broken Nose.

Piebald cows patrol its boundaries
and on a flat down to its right,
there's a mob of Curlews camping,
I hear them singing in the night.

The moon rises past Cairns Inlet
sinking westwards towards the Springs,
while I listen in its golden light,
as each feathered brother sings.

Wondering if I knew them
down beside the Coral Sea,
did they see the concrete suburbs coming,
climb the range and follow me?

Tossy is a little outback Queensland roo who lives with her mate Mad Mick. Tossy is an eastern grey kangaroo whose mother was a road victim so she was reared from a small joey by Mad Mick. When she was found, Tossy's leg was so badly broken that the vet recommended she should be put down. This was unthinkable so we opted to have her leg amputated. Though it was suggested that stress would kill her, she came through. Now **she uses her tail as a leg to walk around** and can hop on one leg with the best of them. Who said Queenslanders aren't resourceful?

Wanita Morrison. The Resourceful Queenslander. Tossy and Mad Mick, Funny Farm, Barcaldine.

Pastel painting by Wanita Morrison

David Sasse

**Colleen McLaughlin.** Running Free. Horses used to muster cattle being released into a paddock of green grass on the completion of a day's work. 'Burnside' **Springsure.** 29 December 2000, 4.30pm.

# We have Freedom.

Freedom from fear,

the fear of not being free.

Freedom to think, to speak, to live

as we wish, within the bounds

of care and concern for those around us.

Freedom from hunger,

freedom to produce

from our Mother Earth

enough. Remembering always

that greed in all things is nemesis.

To be free we must only ask for—

and take—

that which is our share

and not plunder wantonly.

Freedom—and its maintenance—

is the alpha and omega

of our contemporary life.

We must guard it well.

# Partners' Gallery

## Part 2

Golden beaches, golden bodies, golden sunshine, Golden Circle.

Golden Circle Limited 260 Earnshaw Road, Northgate Qld 4013
Phone +61 7 3266 0000 Fax +61 7 3260 5994 www.goldencircle.com.au
Golden Circle is a proud sponsor of Surf Life Saving Queensland.

As well as being a world-class teaching and research institution, The University of Queensland is where students can find lifelong friendships. Many students congregate in the University's beautiful hub, the sandstone-clad Great Court. Basking in Queensland's sub-tropical climate along the banks of the Brisbane River just 7 kilometres from the city's centre, the 90-year-old University boasts three campuses for its more than 30,000 students and 5,000 staff. Among the nation's top four universities, some of its leading facilities include Australia's largest marine station on the Great Barrier Reef, an experimental mine and medical and dental schools.

The University of Queensland Brisbane Qld 4072
Phone +61 7 3365 1111 Fax +61 7 3365 1100 www.uq.edu.au

THE UNIVERSITY
OF QUEENSLAND

197

Ipswich's Global Arts Link is ranked among the **finest public galleries** in Australia, polling number 1 in a study of eastern states galleries in terms of visitation, program attendance and volunteer resources.

The gallery strengthened its reputation by securing 'Two Emperors: China's Ancient Origins' featuring the famous terracotta warriors. Other exhibitions at the state-of-the-art venue have included the original paintings of Ipswich's own d'Arcy Doyle and paintings by John Constable and Thomas Gainsborough from the Art Gallery in Ipswich, in the United Kingdom.

Ipswich City Council 50 South Street, Ipswich Qld 4305
Phone +61 7 3810 6666 Fax +61 7 3810 6731 www.ipswich.qld.gov.au

Standing 197 centimetres tall and weighing 250 kilograms the Terracotta General was discovered in 1977 and excavated from Pit 1 at the Qin Shihuang mausoleum. Collection of Museum of the Qin Shihuang Terracotta Army, Peoples Republic of China.

Ipswich
City Council

Griffith University has an international reputation for teaching and research excellence. With significant links to education institutions and industry partners around the world, including agreements with more than 150 institutions, it is recognised as one of the most creative and influential universities in the Asia-Pacific region. Established in 1971, it is named in honour of Sir Samuel Griffith (1845–1920), a former Premier and Chief Justice of Queensland and the first Chief Justice of Australia.

Karen Kindt, Griffith University

## Griffith University Kessels Road, Nathan Qld 4111

Phone +61 7 3875 7111 www.gu.edu.au

Griffith University Queensland Conservatorium international student Maya Enokida, South Bank Brisbane.

21 November 2001, 5.00pm.

**GRIFFITH UNIVERSITY**

South Bank is the centrepiece of Brisbane's cultural landscape. A creative hub of accessible arts and a mirror for cultural identity—an eclectic blend of students, families, tourists, artists and performers who create an ever changing snapshot of life in the sun. It's a place of many personalities that creates the very identity of Brisbane.

**South Bank Business Association** in conjunction with **South Bank Corporation**

Level 3, South Bank House, Stanley Street Plaza, South Bank Qld 4101

Phone +61 7 3867 2000 Fax +61 7 3844 9436  www.south-bank.net.au

Our thanks to the Queensland College of Art, Photography and Queensland Conservatorium, Griffith University for their assistance with the photograph.

**South Bank**
always creating

Queensland's happening capital stands out among Australian cities, growing at a rate that will see it become Australia's second largest city by 2020. Brisbane's personality and can-do attitude set the city apart. Brisbane is fun, youthful and savvy with a hint of irreverence that's reflected in its lifestyle, business and play. The compact hub of downtown Brisbane is a unique mix of outdoor action, beaches and parklands, tempting menus, happening night-life, seven-day shopping and cultural attractions. Then, less than 60 minutes from downtown Brisbane, so much is so close: from beaches, bay and islands to hinterland, rainforest and country.

Brisbane Marketing Level 12, 15 Adelaide Street, Brisbane Qld 4000
Phone +61 7 3006 6200 Fax +61 7 3006 6250 www.brisbanemarketing.com.au

As surely as night follows day, Ergon Energy and
its people are working around the clock to provide
reliable power to regional Queensland communities.
From the coast to the outback,
Ergon Energy is a key partner in Queensland economic
and social development, delivering creative energy
solutions to meet diverse customer needs.

**People Powering People**

Ergon Energy Pty Ltd 61 Mary Street, Brisbane Qld 4000
Phone +61 7 3228 8222  Fax +61 7 3228 8118  www.ergon.com.au

Quintessential Queensland…shade thrown by a
beautiful old Moreton Bay fig provides a cool place
to bait a line while **enjoying the outdoor
lifestyle** the Sunshine State's renowned for.

Sizzling surf sports are a highlight across Queensland's **fantastic beaches** most weekends. The top competitive surf lifesavers take part in events including ironman, board, ski, surf boats, swim and beach sprints.

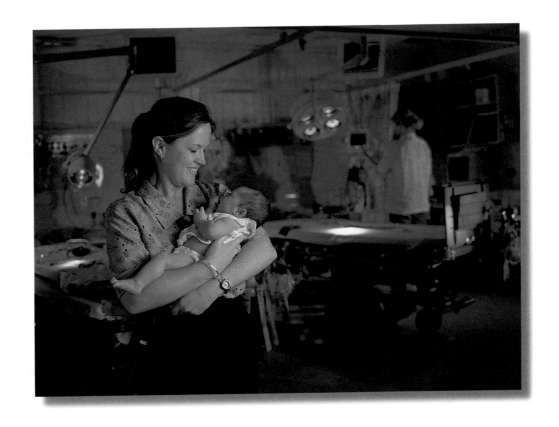

Each year Golden Casket gives away hundreds of millions of dollars in lottery prizes to Queenslanders. Through Golden Casket's Rainbow Kids it also helps put big smiles on thousands of little faces. Golden Casket has a proud history of community support and it continues this tradition today by funding child health initiatives throughout the state.

Golden Casket Lottery Corporation Limited
87 Ipswich Road, Woolloongabba Qld 4102
Phone +61 7 3877 1000 Fax +61 7 3877 1140 www.goldencasket.com

Queensland Investment Corporation (QIC) is one
of Australia's largest wholesale funds managers and
plays an important role in the **financial and
community life of Queensland.**
By providing superior funds management services,
QIC continues to contribute to the wealth of the
state and its people.

Queensland Investment Corporation
Level 6, Central Plaza Two, 66 Eagle Street, Brisbane Qld 4000
Phone +61 7 3360 3800 Fax +61 7 3360 3979 www.qic.com.au

The Main Arena events are a highlight of the August Royal Queensland Show. The Royal Queensland Show, or 'Ekka' as it is affectionately referred to by Queenslanders, is the state's largest annual event, a time when the country comes to town for a 10-day celebration of the 'best of the best' of Queensland.

Royal National Association RNA Showgrounds, Gregory Terrace, Bowen Hills Qld 4006
Phone +61 7 3852 1831 Fax +61 7 3257 1428 www.rnashowgrounds.com.au, www.ekka.com.au

Tarong Energy Corporation Limited is a robust and diverse Queensland Corporation that generates more than a quarter of the state's electricity. As one of the larger regional businesses, we are committed to creating broader opportunities, development and growth for all Queenslanders but especially in the communities in which we operate.

**Tarong Energy Corporation Limited** Level 10, AMP Place, 10 Eagle Street, Brisbane Qld 4001
Phone +61 7 3228 4333 Fax +61 7 3228 4329 www.tarongenergy.com.au

The deaerator feed water tank at the 1,400 megawatt Tarong Power Station performs a pivotal function in the generation process, storing water for the boiler feed pumps. It can hold up to 256 tonnes of water and transfer 300 litres per second.

Queensland's idyllic quality of living is complemented by the quality culture of The Riviera Group, the manufacturer of Australia's **most awarded luxury cruisers.** The company is firmly embracing the future by training 120 apprentices and employing over 550 craftspeople, to produce 350 boats a year. Boats that showcase Queensland ingenuity in 25 export markets worldwide.

The Riviera Group 50 Waterway Drive, Coomera Qld 4209
Phone +61 7 5502 5555 Fax +61 7 5502 5599 www.riviera.com.au

A fantastic journey into worlds of fun where movie magic happens every day, you can meet your favourite marine friends, get wet and go wild … where else but Queensland?

Warner Village Theme Parks

Warner Bros. Movie World, Pacific Highway Oxenford Qld 4210

Phone +61 7 5573 3999 Fax +61 7 5573 8495 www.movieworld.com.au

ABN AMRO Morgans is Australia's leading retail stockbroker. While our network spans the nation, our heart remains in Queensland raising billions of dollars for Queensland companies including Australian Magnesium Corporation, Suncorp Metway and Flight Centre.

ABN AMRO Morgans Ltd
Level 29, Riverside Centre, 123 Eagle Street, Brisbane Qld 4001
Phone +61 7 3334 4888 Fax +61 7 3831 9946 www.abnamromorgans.com.au

Strong, clean and green, 21st century, collaborative, international in focus, committed to value adding, passionate about research and development, at the forefront of new technology… just some of the words used to describe Queensland and Magnesium.

Australian Magnesium Corporation Limited
Level 5, 30 Little Cribb Street, Milton Qld 4064
Phone +61 7 3837 3400 Fax +61 7 3837 3423 www.austmg.com

Bank of Queensland is proud to be an integral part of the Queensland landscape. With Queensland staff and customers, we strive to be a **great Queensland company** moving in step with this dynamic state.

Bank of Queensland 229 Elizabeth Street, Brisbane Qld 4000
Phone +61 7 3212 3333 Fax +61 7 3212 3399 www.boq.com.au

From sunrise to city night lights, the panorama from our River Place apartments is just one example of how Devine's landmark developments are **improving the view of Queensland** for investors around the world.

Devine Limited 3 Westmoreland Boulevard, Springwood Qld 4127
Phone +61 7 3380 2500 Fax +61 7 3380 2370

Dreamworld is helping **Queensland's unique wildlife** by participating in breeding programs for the endangered cassowary —in Australia they are only found in tropical north Queensland.

Dreamworld Dreamworld Parkway, Coomera Qld 4209
Phone +61 7 5588 1111 Fax +61 7 5588 1108 www.dreamworld.com.au

ENERGEX connecting with our customers, **our communities** and our people.

ENERGEX 150 Charlotte Street, Brisbane Qld 4001
Phone +61 7 3407 4000 Fax +61 7 3407 4609 www.energex.com.au

A **breathtaking** encounter with a magnificent humpback whale in Hervey Bay. The photograph was taken by the renowned whale and dolphin photographer Mark Farrell aboard the MV *Whalesong*. Mark was awarded the Suncorp Metway Young Queenslander of the Year in 2001.

George Patterson Bates Queensland's leading Advertising Agency and Creative Consultant to *Queensland by Invitation*.

**Vision to reality.** InterGen's $1.4 billion Millmerran Power project—a long-term commitment to the community and cultural diversity of Queensland.

InterGen (Australia) Pty Ltd Level 18, Comalco Place, 12 Creek Street, Brisbane Qld 4000
Phone +61 7 3001 7177 Fax +61 7 3001 7178 www.intergen.com

Charlene Gordon and Tom Brown, Cultural Heritage Liaison Officers, Millmerran Power representing the Aboriginal groups with cultural links to the site, pictured with Millmerran Mayor, Paul Antonio.

Queenslanders. Work hard. Play hard.

# Love winning.

Macarthur Coal Limited—A Queensland resources company developing a portfolio of new generation coal assets in Queensland's Bowen Basin.

On the lush, misty hills of the Atherton Tablelands the **perfect cup of tea** is slowly brewing.

Nerada Tea Pty Ltd 3/23 Overlord Place, Acacia Ridge Qld 4110
Phone +61 7 3272 0444 Fax +61 7 3272 0243
The Nerada tea plantation set against the backdrop of Mt Bartle Frere, Queensland's highest peak.

Located 170 kilometres north of Roma, Origin's advanced Yellowbank **gas processing facility** saves 700,000 tonnes of greenhouse gas emissions every 4 years—the equivalent to taking 170,000 cars off Queensland's roads for a year.

Origin Energy Limited 339 Coronation Drive, Milton Qld 4064
Phone +61 7 3867 0202 Fax +61 7 3867 0325 www.originenergy.com.au

*delivering the goods*

Hidden Heroes, **heroes like Ron**, quietly go about performing amazing feats, keeping the machines of industry profitable.

**Reliance Worldwide** 40 Ross Street, Newstead Qld 4006
Phone +61 7 3252 3646 Fax +61 7 3252 9391 www.relianceworldwide.com.au

Queenslanders are among the nation's most **experienced water experts,** ensuring the state's vital arteries keep flowing. Snow Engstrom, a SunWater employee, is one such Queenslander.

**SunWater** PO Box 536, Brisbane Qld 4002
536 Albert Street, Brisbane Qld 4002
Phone +61 7 3225 2706 www.sunwater.com.au

A kaleidoscope of colour fills the night skies as **Townsville celebrates** the Centenary of Federation with the Fire & Water Spectacular. This event was the grand finale of the Federation North celebrations to commemorate the Centenary of Federation in 2001.

Andrew Rankin

Townsville Enterprise Limited Enterprise House, 6 The Strand, Townsville Qld 4810
Phone +61 7 4726 2728 Fax +61 7 4726 2700 www.townsvilleonline.com.au
The Strand beachfront. 11 August 2001.

WorkCover supports Queensland.
We aim to balance customer needs, providing the best possible benefits to workers at the lowest cost to employers.

WorkCover Queensland 280 Adelaide Street, Brisbane Qld 4000
Phone 1300 362 128 Fax +61 7 3006 6400 www.workcoverqld.com.au

Since 1924 when Yellow Cabs commenced operation in Brisbane, through times of depression, war, drought and floods, Yellow Cabs has been an **integral part** of Queensland's heritage. In this new century, with a fleet of more than 1,000 cabs using cutting-edge technology, Yellow Cabs is a world model for the taxi industry.

Yellow Cabs (Queensland) Pty Ltd 116 Logan Road, Woolloongabba Qld 4102
Phone +61 7 3391 2008 Fax +61 7 3391 6265 www.yellowcabs.com.au

## FOCUS PUBLISHING
PTY LTD

A FOCUS PUBLISHING BOOK PROJECT
Focus Publishing Pty Ltd
ABN 55 003 600 360
PO Box 518 Edgecliff NSW 2027
Telephone 61 2 9327 4777
Fax 61 2 9362 3753
Email focus@focus.com.au
Website www.focus.com.au
For all enquiries regarding distribution and sales, please
contact the Circulation and Communications Manager.

Project Manager Andra Müller
Senior Editor Diane Jardine
Designer Sarah Cory
Design Concept Deidre Stein
Client Services Kate Sanday, Sophie Beaumont
Production Manager Timothy Ho

Chairman Steven Rich AM
Publisher Jaqui Lane
General Manager (Publishing) Sally Harper
Associate Publisher Gillian Fitzgerald
Corporate Communications Belinda Carson
Circulation and Communications Manager Gloria Nykl
Events Manager Heather Boothroyd

Cover Design George Patterson Bates

Queenland by Invitation
ISBN 1 875359 97 4
Queensland—Description and travel
919.43

For more information on Focus Publishing
visit www.focus.com.au